T

Davıd Krıeger

Poems

The Doves
Flew High

For Mubarak Awad,

With appreciation for
your many acts of peace
rooted in nonviolence —

Best wishes,

David
4/2008

ARTAMO PRESS
SANTA BARBARA · CALIFORNIA

Published by
ARTAMO PRESS

Artamo Press, first edition, 2007
Copyright © 2007 by David Krieger

Artamo Press is a division of Artamo LLC.

Book and cover design by Jack N. Mohr
The cover design is based on a collage by Jack N. Mohr
using a drawing by GUMO (Günter Mohr)

Library of Congress Control Number: 2007928072
ISBN 978-0-9788475-5-5

www.artamopress.com

Printed on acid-free paper in the United States of America

This book is dedicated to all who,
by their passion for peace
and the persistence of their efforts,
make the doves fly high.

ACKNOWLEDGMENTS

I am inspired by individuals throughout the world who have made peace a priority in their lives. Among them, I owe a debt of gratitude to Richard Falk, Frank Kelly, Perie Longo, Mairead Corrigan Maguire, Stuart Rees and Gerry Spence for their encouragement, counsel and friendship. I am also thankful to Vicki Stevenson for her patience and care with the evolving manuscript and her constant good nature. Special thanks to my wife, Carolee, for her support and for caring so deeply.

I am also grateful to Jack N. Mohr and Dr. Elvira Monika Laskowski-Caujolle of ARTAMO PRESS for their care and expertise in publishing this volume. My appreciation also to Monika for helpful suggestions in organizing the book, and to Jack for the book's design and typesetting.

The poems in this volume have nearly all been written in the last two years, a time of war, making the need for peace all the greater. Many of the poems have been included in speeches I have made in many parts of the world, and some have appeared in small peace journals and on peace-related websites.

CONTENTS

CONTENTS

CONTENTS

War is a cowardly escape from the problems of peace.

— Thomas Mann

When I despair, I remember that all through history the way of truth and love has always won. There have been tyrants and murderers and for a time they seem invincible but in the end, they always fall — think of it, always.

— M. K. Gandhi

The Doves Flew High

Poems

How small our voices
in the terrifying din
of wartime lies.

And yet,
how lost this world
would be without
these plaintive cries.

CREDO

CREDO

There are no borders to love or tears.

What we share is the white moon on a cold night,

clouds against the mountains and the clarity of rain.

SEARCHING FOR THE WORDS

I want to write a poem that feeds the hungry,
a poem that makes the world healthy,
one that ends torture
and replaces greed with compassion.

I want to write a poem that awakens people
to the horror of war, a poem that ends our addiction
to violence, one that reveals the obscenity of sending
young men and women to war.

I want to write a poem that defeats nuclearism
and militarism and every other "ism," a poem
that celebrates human dignity and the beauty
and abundance of the earth.

I want to write a poem that brings down leaders
before they commit genocide
and other intolerable crimes, a poem
that ends impunity.

I want to write a poem that celebrates
the miracle of life, one that makes young people aware
of their own beauty and fills them with courage
to fight for justice.

I am searching for the words, the grammar,
the language, the rhythms to write such a poem.
Such words are still forming like cooling lava,
and the rules of grammar are as uncertain as mist.

But the language, the language must be of the heart's pulse.
And the rhythms must be those of the wind and tides.

A poem of such magic cannot be found in books
or on ancient scrolls. Such a poem cannot be written
in stone, or ink or even blood. It can only be lived.

Song of the Seasons

SONG OF THE SEASONS

Come out from behind your spring face,
Your face of sunflowers and dew.

Take a chance on being as real as the red blaze
that tinges the clouds at sunset.

Speak in the lazy lizard tongues of summer,
but only what you know is true.

You will not be here forever before
your autumn face turns brittle and floats away.

Come out from behind your winter wrinkled face,
your tired and lonely face of resistance.

Come out and, for once, be you.

A Still Pond with Water Lilies

After a morning walk,
I sit alone by a still pond.

The pond pulls into itself
reflections of grasses
and adolescent trees.

Dragonflies hover and dart,
chasing each other,
above the deep green water.

There is a slow breathing rhythm
to the quiet perfection
of the moment.

A frog tenses its muscles
and leaps from the grassy bank,
breaking the still, flat water

with a Basho splash.

THE ONE-HEARTED

The one-hearted walk a lonely trail.
They hold the dream of peace between
the moon's eclipse and the rising sun.

They set down their weapons, carrying
instead the spirits of their ancestors,
a collection of smooth stones.

At night, they make fires, and watch
the smoke rise into the starlit sky.

They are warriors of hope, navigating
oceans and crossing continents.

Their message is simple: Now
is the time for peace. It always has been.

THE FLOWERS OF SPRING

We marched for peace through the autumn streets
With a vision of spring in our hearts.

Our numbers swelled as we envisioned the hell
Sure to follow the onset of war.

We did what we could and wished to do more
Knowing what lay in store if we failed.

We marched in the streets and tried to be bold
But in the end the bombs shattered the peace.

While we spoke with our feet on the winter streets
The bombs exploded with force unreserved.

The war left us cold with snow in our hearts
As we witnessed new death unfold undeserved.

Our marching ceased and we left the streets
Watching with grief as the bombs took their toll.

War came again on the wings of a lie
And young men were ordered to kill and to die.

We've come to that place we've regretted before
Where our hopes for peace have fallen to war.

It's a blow to the spirit that tears us apart
While the flowers of spring wither our hearts.

PEOPLE OF THE BOMB

People of the Bomb

It began with fear, not famine.
What was missing was an understanding
of consequences.

Still, the sky held a blue-white innocence.
It would be many years before light
would become so intense that you could see
your bones through translucent skin.

Silos still held grain, not missiles.
Snow-capped mountains brushed the sky
and held it aloft.

The bomb may have ended the war, but only
if history is read like a distant star.

What happened at Hiroshima and Nagasaki
cannot be forgotten, nor easily forgiven.

If only time had not bolted and changed course.
If only the white flags had flown before
the strange storm. If only there had been
one less Einstein and one more Vonnegut.

The sky turned white and aged, then
the colors of daybreak melted our hearts.

LEO SZILARD

Strange little man with slick black hair
and the best of intentions. One day
you intuited the Bomb while waiting
at a red light in London.

Alarmed by the explosion in your mind
you went to your friend Einstein, warning him
it could be a Hitler Bomb. You asked Einstein
to send a letter to Roosevelt.

That was the beginning.

Working under the bleachers at Hutchins' University
you helped give shiny metallic life to your idea, but
your conscience stopped you short when you knew
they were going to drop it. You wrote to Truman
who sent you to Byrnes who scorned you.

You shivered as your train rolled homeward,
knowing you had lost control forever
of your demon child.

LESLIE GROVES

Your photos show you
as a portly, desk-bound
soldier, bulging at the waist,
a fat destroyer of worlds,
who never trusted Szilard
or Oppenheimer.

You fought hard
for using the bomb. You
weren't about to let your
moment in the sun
be eclipsed by the moon
or by the scientists
who had done their jobs,
but knew nothing
of the job of war.

You were proud of what
you had masterminded.
You brought it all together,
and when it was done
you knew the bombs
had to be used,
or all your efforts
would have come
to nothing.

After Trinity

In the week after the Trinity test,
which lit up the early morning sky
with its fierce white power,
Oppenheimer was somber.

Knowing what was soon to follow,
he walked aimlessly about Los Alamos
puffing on his pipe, his eyes vacant.

Over and over, he muttered,
"Those poor little people, those poor
little people."

"Fini Japs"

Truman knew what would end the war.
He wrote it in his diary on July 17, 1945.
He wasn't thinking about the Bomb.
He had Stalin in mind.

Just three weeks before the bombs were dropped,
Truman wrote crudely in his diary:
"He'll be in the Jap war on August 15.
Fini Japs when that comes about."

Jimmy Byrnes, the Secretary of State,
was thinking about Stalin, too.
Byrnes didn't want the Japanese to surrender
to the Soviets. He didn't want to share the spoils.

He wanted the war over before the Soviets
came in. Thus, the terms of surrender
were unconditional, leaving no space
for negotiations, and the secret bombs
were rushed to readiness.

PARALLEL UNIVERSES

If only I had known, I would have become a watchmaker.
— Albert Einstein

In a parallel universe, Einstein
sits at his workbench making watches.
Light still curves around bodies of mass,
but the watchmaker knows nothing of it.
He only makes watches, simple and precise.
In this universe, Hiroshima and Nagasaki
have no special meaning.

Small Possibilities

... within the narrow margin of small possibilities.
— Leo Szilard to Robert Hutchins

They were two dream warriors who, on some days,
thought that the world could be saved.

Szilard, the not-so-mad scientist, Hungarian
immigrant, friend of Einstein, fought for the bomb
and then spent the rest of his life fighting against it.

Hutchins, the tall, eloquent university president, son
of a minister, listened to Szilard's schemes and said,
"Why not?"

Both men lived in a time of change. They were men
of ideas who stood their ground between earth and sky.

They watched as the sphere of reason shriveled and
drifted away, as national security became our religion
and the bomb our favorite god.

August Mornings

August Mornings

Hiroshima

Clear summer morning —
The steel-hearted bomb
Just a speck in the sky

Nagasaki

The bomb shatters
The humid summer silence —
Severs the heads of stone saints

HIROSHIMA

The city wears a cloak of grief
in the air and on the streets,

in the way people move and speak,
in the lights and sounds of the city.

What else must we know about the future
than this: flames and ashes.

It is not enough that flowers have grown
in Hiroshima when so many people have died.

The heat has melted time. Everything is charred.
Even the sunlight is filtered by sadness.

YOSUKE YAMAHATA

The day the bomb fell on Nagasaki, you were there
with your camera, capturing evidence of the crime.

Click. A dying infant sucking at her mother's breast,
the mother's eyes glazed and distant.

Click. A dazed child holding a rice ball, her eyes blank,
her face covered with scratches.

Click. The rigid body of a charred young boy
stretched out and blackened on the crisp earth,

one hand clutching at his chest, the other hand
twisted in a strange way, his face passive.

What were the boy's last words before he turned to clay?
Did he cry out, "Mother, mother"?

Echoes in the Sky

Today the bells of Nagasaki echo in the sky...
— Mayor Iccho Itoh, Nagasaki

The sky, bitter, blue, unyielding, holds promise.
The city, so magical and welcoming, deserved far better.
The clouds opened and made space for devastation.
The people below never knew what happened.

Before anyone expected, the flowers returned.
Memories are painful, sometimes unbearable.
The words of apology never came.
The survivors grow old and feeble.
Generations pass.

The air above the sea is thick with sorrow.
The bells ring out for peace, echoing
in the sky's embrace.

EISENHOWER'S VIEW

It wasn't necessary to hit them with that awful thing.
— General Dwight D. Eisenhower

We hit them with it, first
at Hiroshima and then at Nagasaki —
the old one-two punch.

The bombings were tests really, to see
what those "awful things" would do.

First, of a gun-type uranium bomb, and then
of a plutonium implosion bomb.

Both proved highly effective
in the art of obliterating cities.

It wasn't necessary.

WHERE DID THE VICTIMS GO?

Where else would the victims go but first
into the air, then into the water, then into the grasses,
and eventually into our food?

I speak of the victims incinerated at Hiroshima
and Nagasaki, those too close to the center
who were caught in the heat and fire
of our new power.

I speak of the victims burned away
to their elemental particles, to atoms,
similar to other atoms, let loose into the atmosphere
to drift and fall without volition.

What does this mean? That we breathe our victims,
that we drink them and eat them, without tasting
the bitterness, in our daily meals.

It means there is no way to live without ourselves
becoming in subtle and powerful ways those
we have destroyed.

MEMORY

Memory

Memory, like moist clay, is malleable.
It may be shaped into vessels of myth.
Myth, in turn, engulfs memory.

History is written and rewritten to become
what never was. Leaders become heroic,
countries glorious, and the young patriotic.

With such simple lies, the universe bends.

WHEN I WAS A CHILD

They taught us to pledge allegiance to the flag
and about "our" wars. The Revolutionary War,
the Indian Wars, the Mexican War, the Civil War,
the Spanish-American War, the First and Second
World Wars, the Korean War.

They taught us to glory in victory,
that dropping atomic bombs
on Hiroshima and Nagasaki only added
to that glory. They taught us
that atomic bombs would keep the peace,
to trust our leaders and not to question
their murderous judgments.

They taught us to drop under our desks
and cover our heads. But they also taught us
to read. That was a mistake.

Thus, we came to know that war is not glorious
and nuclear weapons do not keep the peace.
And glorious victories are only won by sending
children to their deaths.

The War Memorial in Brussels

We have much to learn from the moon.
The tides, too, could be our teachers,
if we would but let them.

Instead, we lower our eyes, shuffle our feet
and dance with the god of ignorance.

Look how gracefully he glides through
the town square and over the rolling hills.

We follow breathlessly, as dark shadows
gather. We toast to the future and so soon

forget the past, those bright-eyed boys
whose dreams were crushed on the battlefield.

EMPEROR HIROHITO ON A WHITE HORSE

I swallow my own tears...
— Emperor Hirohito

Surrender has a bitter taste.

Even in this old photograph at the height of empire,
sitting straight on a white horse in his imperial uniform,
a sash across his torso, his sword by his side,
with war medals glittering on his chest,
he appears small and vulnerable.

Emperors and fools leave little space for defeat.

He dismounts from the white horse, carefully puts away
the imperial uniform, the sash, the sword, the medals.

He sits quietly, alone, contemplating the small cup
of tears, as though the cup were filled with hemlock.

REFLECTIONS ON A TRAGIC HISTORY

From sea to shining sea, across the continent,
how can our hearts not be broken in America?

Our Founding Fathers, even those who spoke
of "unalienable rights," were slaveholders.

Riches were amassed on the broken lives
and welted backs of slaves.

In an early act of genocide, we gave
germ-infested blankets to the Indians.

We forced these native peoples onto reservations
and took their lands.

When it came to modern war, we carpet bombed cities,
massacring civilians.

We created atomic weapons and obliterated
Hiroshima and Nagasaki for all the wrong reasons.

We sacrificed our children and slaughtered peasants
for presidential lies.

We invaded and occupied countries and destroyed
lives too numerous to count.

We bestowed medals, sang patriotic songs and wrote glorious histories.

Is there no possibility that our hearts, like sad continents, may reattach themselves to life?

SURRENDER

The barbarians swept past the crumbled city walls,
seizing the highest offices in the land. They rang
the temple bells, but we were deaf to the alarm.

They trained our children in the arts of war
and ferried them to distant lands. Like tin soldiers,
like dominoes, the young soldiers tipped and fell.

Promises fell faster than our youth
but no one raised a voice.

Forgotten now is Orwell, who warned of darkening skies.
Forgotten now is Gandhi, who quietly held his ground.
Forgotten now is King, who thundered out his dream.

How frail our memories, how great our loss.

HOW DARE WE?

HOW DARE WE?

We move so deliberately from the light
into dark shadows, becoming machines
of death, well-oiled, jolting ahead.

We turn our young men into gears, destroying
their human qualities as they, in their sameness,
roll over what stands before them.

We are mighty, so we take what we want
when we want, believing there is no accounting.

We build bombs instead of schools, substituting
brutality for beauty. The edifice of civilization
cracks as we destroy its cradle.

How dare we remain silent when our decency
is being looted before our eyes?

WINSTON SMITH VISITS AMERICA

At the border, the immigration officer checked
Winston's fingerprints and did an eye scan.

A message popped up: Plebe shows
a decided lack of enthusiasm for Hate Week.

A red flag waved.

Winston was cuffed and carted off
for mug shots before being sent

to Guantanamo,

where he was water-boarded,
electroded, brutalized and sodomized.

He was kept in prison without a lawyer,
without charges and without visitors.

The torture never ended, even after he admitted
that he didn't hate the Iraqis, the Iranians,

or anybody,

except Big Brother, who put his black boot
down so calmly on Winston's screaming face.

WARNING TO AMERICANS

If you want a picture of the future, imagine a boot
stamping on a human face — forever.
— George Orwell, 1948

Don't look in the mirror. You may be frightened
by the raw redness of your jingoism. You may find
a flag tattooed on your forehead or on your chest.

Don't talk about victory. The words that tumble
from your mouth will be irretrievable.
Your children will know how you exalted in death.

Don't mourn the loss of your freedoms. Remember,
Orwell warned this day would come.
Your freedoms were not meant to last forever.

Don't become disoriented or lose your bearings
as our Little Fool is transfigured into Big Brother.
He is there for you and you for him.

Don't allow yourself to think about another world
for that would demand your resistance. Remember,
you were silent as Orwell's world took seed and grew thorns.

Don't be alarmed when you read reports from the battlefield
as we follow the flag from country to country. Remember,
war is glorious for those who wear the polished black boot.

War in a Time of Cowardice

Lessons learned from Vietnam

Begin with lies, the bolder the better. Diagrams
are helpful.

Dump the draft. Promise the poor an education
after they serve.

Tell the people that the war will either save democracy
or spread it.

Claim victory or argue it is right around the corner.

Don't do body counts. Hide the body bags.

Use fewer troops, and bomb from high altitudes.

Don't allow photos of the returning coffins.

Keep lying.

New Rules

Fight preventive wars at a time of our choosing.

International law is irrelevant.

You are either with us or with the enemy.

Embed the press.

Detain prisoners indefinitely, without rights.

Authorize torture, then blame the soldiers
who administer it.

If in doubt, swagger.

To an Iraqi Child

— for Ali Ismail Abbas

So you wanted to be a doctor?

It was not likely that your dreams
would have come true anyway.

We didn't intend for our bombs to find you.

They are smart bombs, but they didn't know
that you wanted to be a doctor.

They didn't know anything about you
and they know nothing of love.

They cannot be trusted with dreams.

They only know how to find their targets
and explode in fulfillment.

They are gray metal casings with violent hearts,
doing only what they were created to do.

It isn't their fault that they found you.

Perhaps you were not meant to be a doctor.

ON SEEING CHICK STREETMAN'S PLAY

It was a play about loss, notes of loved ones
left at the Vietnam War Memorial.
The names on that polished black granite Wall
came to life with messages from the living,
the saddest from the children the dead men
never knew. I thought about those who lied
to send these youngsters off to face their deaths,
and the politicians who are doing it again,
as though they'd learned nothing from the Wall.

Different places, Vietnam and now Iraq —
some died in jungles, some in arid deserts,
some from roadside bombs. In the end,
what is left are memories and pain, and names
carved in a granite wall. Not much,
but better than nothing at all, a record
of how we failed our children yet again.

QANA STREET SCENE

And the blood of children ran through the streets.
— Pablo Neruda

There are scenes too horrible
to imagine or dream. Yes, this is our world.
We slaughter infants in our wars in the most
gruesome ways. No need to leave such horror
to our imaginations. It plays on the nightly news.

Of course, no one purposely kills infants.
It just happens. Soldiers are not good
at their craft, nor are politicians at theirs.
Rather than diplomacy, soldiers fire rockets
and drop bombs from the blue sky.

There is blood on our hands, blood all around.
Small, thin arms stream blood. Blood flows
from collapsed lungs. There is nowhere
to hide, nowhere to play, nowhere to pray
and no redemption left.

On the Third Anniversary of the Iraq War

A lonely hawk soars in an azure sky,
oblivious to the folly of men.

The breeze shakes through the sycamores,
new leaves signaling spring.

Fields of nasturtiums, orange and red, ripple
in the wind. Birds chatter in the trees.

Men in high office make it their work
to destroy such beauty.

On this day of despair, this third anniversary
of a senseless war, there is still

not a single weapon of mass destruction
to be found.

THE OTHER SIDE
OF THE WORLD

The Other Side of the World

In this sacred place defined by water, gentle
breezes and the sounds of birds, a lone kayaker
paddles across the shimmering bay toward
the horizon. This is one side of the world.

On the other side, bombs are falling on cities
blowing up children and other innocents
for the sake of vengeance or peace or
whatever reason. For the mothers

there is nothing but the cold terror
of the silver planes unloading
their lethal cargo, and the anguish
of losing those they love.

On the other side of the world, the young pilots
and their crews do with deadly precision
only what they were so well trained to do.

ANOTHER SOLDIER

The fifteen hundredth American soldier has died
in an ancient land.

I don't know his name, nor can I imagine his face,
surprised or perhaps contorted, as he fell like an anchor
through the sea.

Like all of us, he had dreams.

We are seized by the penetrating beauty of flowers,
by their arrangement in a crystal vase, and cannot help
sinking to the sad earth.

When the flowers, too, have faded and fallen,
the empty container will remain solid and solitary,
reflecting light, but lifeless and achingly alone.

Twenty Years of War

Ours is a geography of fear, a world
of ghosts, interrogation rooms, corrupt
authorities and mingled bones.

As much as we may wish it, there is no
shining path. The space for withdrawal
or surrender narrows.

Sad trails wind up and down snow covered
mountains. In the weighty silence, the dead,
half-dead and tortured are ever present.

Gravity pulls on recurring nightmares,
as women hide trembling
behind thick walls and iron gates.

Shards of truth are unearthed, examined
and discarded. Old generals, defiant, brace
themselves to hold their bloody ground.

But the people, one by one, find courage
and each other in the streets. They rush
like water, against the thirsty walls of war.

ARGENTINA

I flew across the night to a land
of brave mothers and poets,
the land of Che and Borges
and the Plaza de Mayo.

The land had busy cities
and a beautiful dark sky.
It had cars and trains
and its share of happiness.

As luck would have it,
I met an old man, stooped and frail.
The old man looked across a wide
and brutal century,

a century of Chagall and Einstein
and too many tragedies.
He recalled the famous
white-haired Russell, who whispered

in his ear as startled doves
flew by, as continents writhed.
The old man knew many sad songs
of war and loss, but he refused to sing.

AN OLD MAN

An old man awakens in the dark night.
His mouth is filled with bitter stars and solitude.
He is disoriented, uncertain of whose world
he has entered.

In his reptile brain, he is afraid.
He shivers, then screams, but no one hears him.
He is unshaven. His white hair is disheveled.
He is dressed only in his black shadow.

He is not at ease with his bones and flesh.
But unlike you, or even me, he is
an imaginary character, entirely fictional.
His face and his past are still undefined.

He may have been someone important
or someone quite ordinary.
It is doubtful he was a hero.

We do not know, nor does he, whether
he was a good man or a brave one.
He lives within dreams and rarely emerges.

It is his responsibility to be who he is.
It is our responsibility to treat him kindly,
to help him become real.

The Sadness of Empire

As the imperial capital prepares for summer
it is blanketed with images of Zarqawi's head.

The disembodied head looks gentle in death,
floating like a lonely white moon.

Look at this head of a terrorist.
What is there to fear from such a head?

The capital buzzes with excitement,
a great victory for the president.

In the halls of Congress they say this head
will be a turning point in the war.

The president dreams of bin Laden's head
rolling on the White House lawn.

In the capital a terrorist's head brings hope,
but it is not the same everywhere.

In Guantanamo, on the other side of the moon,
three prisoners place their heads in nooses,
flex their knees and jump toward heaven.

Approaching 2,500 American Deaths in Iraq

A crow sits on a wire fence, staring
into thick fog.

In Iraq, suicide bombings increase.
The numbers vary, but each day
there are more deaths, mostly Iraqis.

One day there are 17 dead, another day 30.
On a very bad day there may be 100 or more.

And the trial of Saddam continues.
The hawk-eyed judge stares down at Saddam.
He wants to know whether Saddam pleads *guilty*.

Saddam says there are no short answers.
The judge interprets this as *not guilty*.

The war drags on; the death toll mounts. But
the dead are hidden from view to save the president
from being embarrassed by such untidiness.

He swaggers as though he knows enough about war,
although he knows nothing of it. The fog closes
around him, engulfs him.

New Year's Eve

As the old year slips away,
a shroud of death covers the moon.

The old year cannot hold Saddam,
hung by the neck, his body twitching,
his shadow spreading across Baghdad
and stretching to Washington.

Beneath Saddam's shadow, Iraq shudders
in pain. Death is everywhere.

Three thousand Americans are dead in Iraq.
Hundreds of thousands of Iraqis are dead
in this war without purpose.

Across America, flags fly at half-mast
for a dead president.
They hardly stir in the dark wind
that sweeps away memory.

Tears
from the Night Sky

TEARS FROM THE NIGHT SKY

The bitter blue tears of Captain Cook fall
from the night sky.

Far away from this lava and green-sea haven
men make senseless war.

First one attack against the innocent
and then another.

The world is not safe for bystanders,
not anywhere.

In our arrogance, we are squandering
the light of the moon and distant stars.

We have lost our bearings on Earth,
our sense of decency and honor.

Look to the far end of the Big Dipper's cup
and follow it to the North Star.

Let the tears from Captain Cook's eyes
wash over your sad and wounded hearts.

Then step out from behind the barricades
and begin the long journey home.

A DAY LIKE ANY OTHER DAY

It was just a day like any other day.
The only thing that made it significant
was that the masses of the people joined in.
— Rosa Parks

By not moving, you began a movement,
like a cat stretching. Then suddenly alert.

By remaining seated, you stood for decency,
though your knees must have trembled.

By rejecting the law, you accepted a higher law,
knowing precisely what you were doing.

By praying silently, you spoke eloquently
in a language ordinary people could understand.

By closing your eyes, you opened ours,
and we could see the path ahead.

By whispering No, you shouted Yes,
and we felt your pain.

By holding your ground, you changed
our course, and we were never the same.

STANDING WITH PABLO

I have a higher duty to my conscience...
— Pablo Paredes

Like the three tenors, like three pillars,
there are three Pablos for peace:
Picasso, Neruda and Paredes.

The first painted Guernica, the second
wrote poems as an act of peace.
The third refuses to fight in Iraq.

There is talk about the conscience of mankind.
But there is no such thing, only
the conscience of each individual.

Pablo Picasso painted the horrors of war.
Pablo Neruda wrote poems of love and decency.
Pablo Paredes refused to kill or be killed.

The three Pablos are comrades against arms.
They stand together for human dignity.
Should we not stand with them?

I Refuse

— for Camilo Mejia

I refuse to be used as a tool
of war.

I refuse to kill on order.

I refuse to give my life for a lie.

I refuse to be indoctrinated
or subordinated.

I refuse to allow the military to define
all I can be.

I refuse to abdicate my responsibilities
as a citizen of the world.

I refuse to deny the human rights
of any person.

I refuse to suspend my conscience.

I refuse to give up my humanity.

I refuse to be silenced.

Do you hear me?

A LITERAL READING

Thou shalt not kill.

Shiny trinkets and ribbons on the chest
are war's sullen rewards.

War is a bloody business, like falling
though a trap door into hell.

Sometimes the truth is too close to us
and we miss its outlines.

Yet, all is not lost: Even the gods
can begin again.

Order Does Not Order Itself

For Einstein, creation was too beautiful and orderly
to be random. God, he was certain, does not roll dice.
The planets follow patterns, large looping patterns

through space. The earth rotates around the sun,
the moon around the earth. The whole universe
follows patterns, no matter who is looking at it.

It is its own universe, petulant but predictable.

Water falls from the sky, and wind sweeps
through the trees. People come and go and live
their only lives. Einstein was one of these people.

He scribbled equations, trying his best to decipher
God's order. He wanted an equation that explained
everything — all the laws of nature.

In the end, he failed. There was no E equals MC squared
for everything. But what a fine time he had trying.

THE DOVES FLEW HIGH

THE DOVES FLEW HIGH

What if they gave a war and no one came?

The president stood before Congress
and, as presidents do, called for war.

The members of Congress, oblivious
to their duties, jumped to their feet cheering.

When he was ready, the president gave the order
for war in his most commanding voice.

But no soldiers were there to receive it —
no general, no colonel, no captain,
no sergeant, no private, no soldier at all.

The young men and women stayed in school
or at their work, voting with their bodies
against war.

The Congress was somber and sober.
Without soldiers, they matured.

The president, devoid of options, chose peace.
And the doves flew high.

NEW YEAR'S DAY

Each New Year carries promise
that we will not be swallowed whole
by the brutality of the year gone by.

Today we hiked Romero trail
puffing up the long sunny dirt road
that looks out to the ocean
then down the cool shaded footpath
by the flowing creek.

It was a happy walk
full of the newness of the year.
Carolee picked white sage to give
our house a ritual cleansing.

When we reached the bottom
of the trail, back to where we started,
we were happy and tired.

For that short while, the war
was far away in another world.

Sisyphus with Bombs: A Modern Myth

Each day from dawn to dusk Sisyphus strained
under his load of heavy bombs as he struggled
up the mountain. It was slavish, back-breaking work.
He sweated and groaned as he inched his way
toward the top of the mountain.

Always, before he reached the top, the bombs
were taken from him and loaded onto bomber aircraft.
Sisyphus would stand and wipe his brow as he watched
the planes take off into the darkening sky on their way
to destroy yet more peasant villages somewhere far away.

Sisyphus believed that he was condemned by fate
to carry the bombs up the mountain each day of his life.
Since he never reached the top, each sunrise he began anew
his arduous and debilitating task.

Strangely, Sisyphus was happy in his work, as were those
who loaded the bombs onto the planes and those who dropped
the bombs on peasant villages. As Sisyphus often repeated,
"It is a job and it fills my days."

Sisyphus with bombs contributes his labors to the war system,
as so many of us do. Let us work to disarm Sisyphus
and give him back his rock. Our reward will be saving
peasant villages and their inhabitants from destruction
and the world from annihilation. By our efforts, we may
even save ourselves. It is the Sisyphean task of our time.

GREAT TRUTH HAS GREAT SILENCE

The small truth has words that are clear;
the great truth has great silence.
— Rabindranath Tagore

When light races across the universe
it runs on silent feet.

While night stretches its dark wings across
the sky, the moon is enveloped in silence.

As trees grow toward the sky and dance
in the wind, their roots sink silently.

In the deepest reaches of the forest, where
no birds call, there is silence.

When fine minds commune across time
and space, thoughts travel silently.

Where love is strong, there is no need
for words.

Within the awful shattering chaos of war,
lives a still and silent seed of peace.

PIONEER VALLEY

MW01279931

MARTIN
LUTHER KING, JR.

MICHÈLE DUFRESNE

TABLE OF CONTENTS

Dr. Martin Luther King, Jr.
was a leader
of the civil rights movement
in the United States.

➤ Dr. Martin Luther King at the podium giving a
   speech in Montgomery, Alabama, after the Selma to
   Montgomery Civil Rights March.

Martin Luther King, Jr. was born on January 15, 1929. He lived in a big house with his grandparents, parents, brother, and sister. His grandfather and father were pastors at a church in Georgia.

➤ Dr. Martin Luther King, Jr.'s birthplace

5

When Martin was growing up,
black people did not have
the same rights
as white people.
Many black children
could not go
to the same schools
as white children.

This is called segregation.

Martin went to college when he was only 15 years old.

After college, he went to school to become a minister.

Then he went to Boston University, where he met Coretta Scott.

➤ The King family in the study of Ebenezer Baptist Church in Atlanta in 1966.

Dr. King married Coretta,
and they had four children.
He became the pastor
at a church
in Montgomery, Alabama.

In many places,

black people did not have

the same rights

as white people.

Dr. King wanted black

people and white people

to be treated equally.

He talked to many people

about using peaceful ways

to end segregation.

▲ On March 21, 1965, Dr. King and other civil rights leaders march for voter registration rights for blacks.

Dr. King did not think
it was right that black people
had to sit at the back
of the bus.
He asked people
to stop riding the buses
to protest peacefully.

In Montgomery, black people
did not ride the bus
for over a year.

In November 1956,
the Supreme Court ruled
that making black people
sit at the back of the bus
was not legal.

There were many laws
that treated black people unfairly.
One law stated that black people
could not sit at lunch counters
with white people.

Dr. King did not think
this was right.

There were peaceful protests
in many cities in the U.S.
that helped change the rules
about where black people
were allowed to sit
at lunch counters.

Some people did not want to
change how black people
were treated. They were angry.
Dr. King was put in jail
many times because he
wanted all people
to be treated equally.

On August 28, 1963,
in Washington D.C.,
Dr. King gave a speech
about a dream he had.

He said he dreamed
that all men
would someday be brothers.
He wanted black people
and white people
to have equal rights.

▲ Martin Luther King Jr., gives his "I Have a
Dream" speech during the Freedom March in
Washington, DC, on August 28, 1963.

After a while,
new laws were passed
to end segregation.

Then one very sad day,
on April 4, 1968,
Martin Luther King, Jr.
was shot and killed.

To honor his life and work, we celebrate his birthday in January each year.

1929 Born January 15

1944 Graduates from Booker T. Washington High School in Atlanta, Georgia

1948 Is ordained to the Baptist ministry February 25

1953 Marries Coretta Scott and moves to Montgomery, Alabama

1955 Joins the bus boycott after Rosa Parks was arrested

1956 The Supreme Court rules that bus segregation is illegal

1958 The U.S. Congress passes the first Civil Rights Act since the Reconstruction

1963 Makes his famous "I Have a Dream" speech in Washington, D. C.

1964 Is awarded the Nobel Peace Prize

1965 The Voting Rights Act becomes a law

1968 Is shot and killed by James Earl Ray April 4